N

HAWAII
IS A GARDEN

HAWAII IS A GARDEN

PETER JACKA

David Bateman Ltd.
Hawaiian Service, Inc.

Dedication

For Mary-Anne who praises every single painting I produce.

Acknowledgements

To all the unknown land and home owners where I found so many of my subjects. I would also like to thank those very knowledgeable people at the Arboretum, Waimea Falls Park who have made such a wonderful contribution to the beauty of that park, which has been an inspiration to me. Thank you all so very much.

© Peter Jacka 1983

First Published in 1983 by
David Bateman Ltd., "Golden Heights"
30-34, View Road, Glenfield, Auckland, New Zealand
and distributed in the U.S.A. by
Hawaiian Service Inc.,
P.O. Box 2835, Honolulu, Hawaii 96803.

ISBN 06-930492-17-X

Typeset in 12 on 14 Korinna by Jacobson Typesetters Ltd
Printed in Hong Kong by Colourcraft Ltd.
Design by Peter Jacka.

Contents

Introduction

"What is that wonderful fragrance?" I asked the porter at the Honolulu airport.

"Oh, Plumeria, I guess. Flowers," he smiled.

And so it was. The perfume of flowers was everywhere. Girls were draping garlands of them around people, kissing, laughing, looking friendly and warm and lovely. There were flowers in their hair and their arms trailed vibrant, scented circles of a hundred different varieties. It was January 1977 and my wife Mary-Anne and I had arrived in paradise to live a life of retirement from New Zealand.

Here we were at last, being greeted by a balmy tropical air ladened with intoxicating fragrances. Showering trees and shrubs ablaze with exotic blooms are everywhere in Hawaii. Wherever you go, wherever you look there are flowers of vivid colors creating a heady perfume that is the islands and is carried aloft on the trade winds and becomes part of your daily life. Mention "Hawaii" and you think flowers. Hawaii is simply one huge garden. The people living here surround themselves with its beauty at every chance, even the most modest dwelling will have its plumeria and hibiscus, its ginger or allamanda. Everything grows so easily and with almost unbelievable vigor. Flowers are a truly wonderful contribution to the islands happy, gentle life style. If you've never seen massed bougainvillea growing wild along a roadside or on a hilly slope, or seen towering hedges twenty feet high smothered in a million hibiscus blooms, then you've never seen Hawaii.

I suppose I have had an affinity for gardens for as long as I can remember. As a boy of eight or nine I was part of gardening groups at school and was encouraged to share my father's enthusiasm for growing things. There's just something about working in a garden and developing natural beauty that, for me, is completely satisfying.

Around our hillside home, looking down on the reef, the surf and the blue of the Pacific, I have planted dozens of bougainvillea, oleander, hibiscus, allamanda, bananas, and flowering shrubs and trees that bloom the year round. Everything seems to have grown so quickly that it looks as if it has been there forever. That is Hawaii — it grows all things beautiful. A garden indeed.

My wife, Mary-Anne, to my surprise, bought me a set of paints for Christmas 1977. I put them aside for several months believing that if I couldn't paint a masterpiece first up, painting wasn't for me! Well I didn't paint a masterpiece though I have always admired watercolors — I guess it's my English heritage. They have a translucency and freshness that has great appeal to me. After endless hours of study under professionals I have been able to develop a style that I enjoy and, judging by sales, the public loves. I have attempted to get the strength and color of oils from watercolors, and feel I have been successful.

In the meantime, Mary-Anne has become an acknowledged fashion designer in Hawaii and not only sells at the top end of the island's market place, but is shown by some of America's great stores in New York, Miami and California. She has also become my most enthusiastic supporter. "That's just beautiful," says Mary-Anne to each and every painting I complete, "we'll keep that one for home."

I have really enjoyed painting for this book and wish my publisher could have authorized twice the number of pages so that I could take an even broader look at the flowers and buildings and trees that make these gentle islands the most beautiful place in the world. Maybe we'll do another one soon.

Honolulu. 1982.   Peter Jacka.

The Royal Hawaiian Hotel is probably the most photographed building in Hawaii. I've painted it several times. I think this is the scene I like best — out in the garden courtyard at night with the lanterns lit and the glow of light across the lawns. When I first came to Hawaii, ''The Royal'' was one of the biggest buildings in Honolulu. Just look at it now! Dwarfed by towering highrises, yet it still seems to hold its own as one of our prettier landmarks. Thank goodness it is being protected.

I used to think these trees were just a rampant weed, but when you see them flowering so perfectly they are then most attractive. The "Angel's Trumpet" is usually white and green but this tree's blooms merged into a delicate apricot which made me want to paint it.

There are many fine buildings in Hawaii but the State Capitol must surely be one of its most graceful. I never fail to take our visitors to see it in its elegance.

Behold! The Kokia Cookei! From the Hibiscus family
— the only one left in the islands. It was grafted from a
specimen on the island of Molokai and I found it at the
Arboretum at Waimea Falls. The plant on Molokai was
burnt and died so this is the only one in Hawaii. The only
other specimen is from grafted stock sent by the
Arboretum to world famous Kew Gardens in England.

I've been going back to Waimea Falls time after time,
year after year and every visit see something new. I wander
off the beaten tracks a lot but when I get a bit puffed I flag
down the trolley and ride for a while in shade and comfort.

The Honolulu Academy of Arts is a building of true Hawaiian influence
and charm. Inside it opens out into delightful courtyards
and I return constantly to the Academy
for its peace and great
charm.

I've wandered through the Polynesian Cultural Center many times; it is alive with all the cultures of the Pacific. The smiling charm of the people there always enchants me. So does the extraordinary power of the color in the Crotons. They always look hand painted to me.

This exotic vine is called Thumbergia and hangs in profusion from trees, even in shady places. What a remarkable shape the bloom is! The old Mission House in Honolulu is an immaculate example of its era. Gleaming white, pristine, simply beautiful. I really enjoy painting these buildings. Its clean white weatherboards remind me of New England. The original residents' furnishings and belongings are still inside the house.

The statue of King Kamehameha I The Great is the focal point of Hawaiian celebrations and proudly stands in front of the Judiciary Building in Honolulu. At these times the king is decked with garlands of flowers and leis and makes an impressive and colorful show for visitors.

The Iolani Palace has been the home of the Hawaiian Monarchs since King Kalakaua took up residence there in 1882. Its style and regal appearance intrigue me. I like to get in close and paint its majestic entrance and lamps and broad steps and huge windows and doors. The pavilion in the gardens is where King Kalakaua was crowned along with his beautiful Queen Kapiolani. The pavilion, or bandstand, is decorated with The Standards of the Kingdom of Hawaii which I show on page 42.

There are many, many different species of ginger all over Hawaii. The flaming red ginger is the most common and can be seen everywhere you go. I painted this scene outside an old Haleiwa country store. Every quaint little home along the way seems to have a vivid display. It's probably one of the most popular flowers in the State.

I painted the tower of the St. Peter and Paul Mission many times as a student. It sits atop a sunny cliff benignly looking down on the spectacular surf and seas that roll in to Waimea Bay. Father Clyde tells me the tower was once used for loading crushed stone when the building was a stone quarry. I have Stephanotis trained along my lanai. It's waxy and beautiful with a tremendous perfume.

22

Many of my color sketches generate paintings. I have dozens of small books filled
with tiny water colors that I have done on site during my wanderings through the islands.
I may render six or seven different color sketches for each subject that I will finally complete
— then I plan them out, change them around, "construct" them in a way that pleases
me and completes the finished painting. Sometimes I get myself buried deep inside my
subject — as I did for the sugar cane plantation painting on the following page.

You really can't have a book about flowers in Hawaii without a page on Impatiens. Everywhere there is a little shade you'll see them. They flower right through the year in a profusion of pinks and reds and mauves.

Overleaf I have painted Bougainvillea, and I had never seen so many different colors of Bougainvillea until I came to Hawaii. Coral ones, red ones, white ones, magenta, gold, mauve, purple — they go on and on. You see them trimmed into shapes, as hedges, wild along roadsides, blazing their way up hills and mountains, blooming all the year round. They need little attention or even much water. Bougainvillea enjoys more comment from visitors possibly than any other flower in the State.

The Banyan is a tree of power and strength. Its vigorous aerial root system stretches down from above and moves across the ground to embrace anything in its path. These mighty trees are a strong attraction for artists.

29

30

Peter Jacka

Look at this superb Stag Horn Fern!
It was propagated half way up a huge
Monkeypod Tree. Look at the way it
curves and sweeps — each leaf a joy in
itself. The semi-sun and shade it thrives in
seems to be environmentally perfect for it.

At parks and beaches I come across cool and shady shelter areas
which I often used to sketch or paint under.

Peter Jaeke

I never seem to see Oleander in flower books and I can never understand why. This single pink has superb form and color. There are rampant trees of it all over the islands. I saw this one at Lahaina on Maui, a quaint little town that always reminds me of a movie set.

The tonal depth of the Ti is something special. It changes with the light from one hour to the next and the reds alter with the seasons. I have them throughout my garden and there are many fine examples in the public gardens and parks throughout the islands.

36

Chinaman's Hat, a tiny island, claims the attention of everyone who tours the windward side of Oahu.

This church on the Kona Coast on the Big Island recalls times long ago when every village had its own church. This charming example symbolizes the peace and serenity which is the way of life in these islands.

Opposite: Butterfly Pea

41

The Standards of The Kingdom of Hawaii are quaint, decorative pieces I noticed on the bandstand in the grounds of the Iolani Palace — a charming, Victorian styled pavilion in which King Kalakaua celebrated his coronation. I have sketched the whole bandstand on page 18. Britain's Union Jack in the corners of the shields intrigues me. So does the pomp and regal atmosphere the Standard conveys.

On the previous page I have painted Birds of Paradise.

Anthuriums always look to me as if they've been sculptured out of wax. The garden shop I go to had this bed of reds and white growing in their shade house.

Allamanda smothers my driveway gardens. I have difficulty capturing its vivid yellows. It's a wonderfully rounded shape which is great to draw. A full, happy flower that suits Hawaii beautifully.

44

Certainly one of the loveliest scents in Hawaii is that of Plumeria, called Frangipani in other islands of the Pacific. Its blossoms are used for the leis which are so identified with these islands. I have painted the whitish cream variety here but they also come in various shades of scarlets and oranges.

It is amazing how much land is covered by plantations on an island as small as Oahu. You drive through them mile after mile yet still find small village gardens tucked away in sleepy valleys. I found this Taro patch just a stone's throw from the main road on the Windward side. Time seemed to have stood still for generations as the field workers harvested their crop. The awesome backdrop of the towering Koolaus capped a perfect scene.

Peter Jacka 49

These amazing giant lily leaves are a focal point at lovely Waimea Falls Park. They tell me the leaves grow to nearly seven feet across! The lily pond is the loveliest I've seen. The pink, red and yellow lilies splash reflective color across the water as decorative accessories to the ''Victoria Amazonica''.

I couldn't believe my eyes the first time I saw the "Showers" in bloom. Gold, pink and creams, pinks and corals. These massive trees burst upon Hawaii around June in showers and showers of fragrant blossom. The trees are big, about thirty, maybe forty feet high. They have an exquisite perfume too and what a sight they are as their petals fall and the trees surround themselves with a carpet of blossom. I was in Waikiki when this one was out doing some color sketches of Diamond Head. "The Diamond" is, of course, our most famous landmark — it seems to change in color and shape as you move around it.

I make no apologies for painting Hibiscus both on the previous page and the title page. I never tire of the grace and beauty of its many forms. Each flower may bloom only briefly but its constant renewal seems to epitomize Hawaiian life.

Thank you, Hawaii.
Aloha